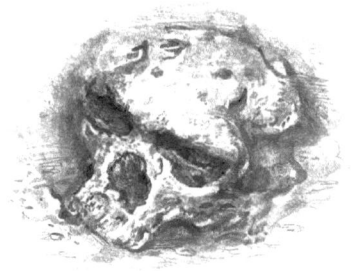

of Species

JOEL BETTRIDGE

DOS MADRES
2024

DOS MADRES PRESS INC.
P.O. Box 294, Loveland, Ohio 45140
www.dosmadres.com   editor@dosmadres.com

Dos Madres is dedicated to the belief that the small press is essential to the vitality of contemporary literature as a carrier of the new voice, as well as the older, sometimes forgotten voices of the past. And in an ever more virtual world, to the creation of fine books pleasing to the eye and hand.

Dos Madres is named in honor of Vera Murphy and Libbie Hughes, the "Dos Madres" whose contributions have made this press possible.

Dos Madres Press, Inc. is an Ohio Not For Profit Corporation and a 501 (c) (3) qualified public charity. Contributions are tax deductible.

Executive Editor: Robert J. Murphy

Book Design: Elizabeth H. Murphy
www.illusionstudios.net
Cover painting: Joe Biel

Typeset in Adobe Garamond Pro & Calton Elegance Script
ISBN 978-1-962847-00-1
Library of Congress Control Number: 2024930748

First Edition
Copyright 2024 Joel Bettridge
All rights reserved. No part of this book may be reproduced or transmitted in any form or by any means graphic, electronic or mechanical, including photocopying, recording, taping or by any information storage or retrieval system, without the permission in writing from the publisher.
Published by Dos Madres Press, Inc.

GRATITUDE

I read widely while writing these poems, but *The Last Human: A Guide to Twenty-Two Species of Extinct Humans*, created by G. J. Sawyer and Viktor Deak, with text by Esteban Sarmiento, G. J. Sawyer, and Richard Milner, was particularly helpful and engaging. Also, for the poems involving creation myths I drew on material included in Barbara Sproul's *Primal Myths*, Diana Ferguson's *Native American Myths*, and Donna Rosenberg's *World Mythology*. As always, thanks to the loved ones whose ongoing conversation, work, and insightful reading of my own, continues to give me the material out of which to make poems: Rebecca Brown, Sam Chambers, Kim Evans, Nathan Goldberg, Peter O'Leary, Roberto Tejada and Joe Biel. I'm especially grateful to Richard Deming for reading many versions of the manuscript and pushing me to make it stronger—he is the better maker. Thanks to my son, Ben Bettridge, for the walks and talks that led to many of these poems and whose humor and curiosity makes each day a joy to share with him. Thanks to Liz Ceppi who knew what to cut from this book and what to keep, and whose presence beside me allows me to know where I am in the world. Lastly, thanks to Debra Gwartney and Barry Lopez whose friendship, writing, and hospitality each summer provided the fertile ground for this project. May the memory of Barry and the continued reading of his work be a blessing to us all.

Table of Contents

HORSES (Author's Introduction) xi

Transmutation I

Transmutation: Kith and Kin 1
Adaptation 2
Craving 3
The Inheritance of Archaeology 4
The Rise of Nation States 5
Spacetime 6
A System of Signs, or Its Forebear,
    Back in the Head of This *Australopithecus* 7
Coasts 8
Pearyland 9

Transmutation II

Transmutation: Laughter 13
Of Prophets and Prophecies 14
Aubade 15
Lucy's Tanka: "I Am Not the Moon" 16
Interlocutor 17
Pantheon 19
The *Homo sapiens* Called Isaac 20
First Version 21
Of Organisms and Not Specimens 22

Transmutation III

Transmutation: Art. 25
Armaments. 26
Homo habilis, in Chorus. 27
Of Erosion and Starting Out 28
Like Schools of Fish Wheeling in the Air 29
The *Homo sapiens* Called Ishmael 31
Learning How to See 32
Mass & Heat 33
The *Homo sapiens* Called Rebekah 34

Transmutation IV

Transmutation: Bears 37
A Theory of Tools. 38
Then This *Homo habilis*, the First Rückenfigur 39
Lessons from the Wolverine 40
One of Some *Homo habilis*. 41
Climate-lapse. 42
The Origin of Biography (*Homo georgicus*) 43
Not Quite Metamorphosis. 44
Second Version. 45
Homo georgicus Continued—Her at a Vanishing Point . . . 46

Transmutation V

Transmutation: Rites 49
A Dream of Empire 50
The *Homo sapiens* Called Jacob. 51
Sister of Needles. 52
Psalms 53

The Love of Deserts 57
Some *Homo georgicus* Going Here and There 58
Boxing the Compass. 59
The Discovery of Grief (*Homo georgicus*). 60

Transmutation VI

Transmutation: Music 63
Tectonic Shifts 64
A Family Tree (*Homo pekinensis*). 65
In Place of an Altar. 66
Thresholds 67
Third Version 68
The *Homo sapiens* Called Rachel. 71
Why Do Islands Swim? 72
Understory. 73

Transmutation VII

Transmutation: History 77
Animals That Did Not Make It into the ARK 78
Crow's Side of the Tale, pastel, graphite on paper
    by Rick Bartow, 1991. 80
The *Homo sapiens* Called Leah 81
Nocturne. 82
Virgil's 81st Grandson Sits in the Tundra. 83
Additional Mammals 84
Minyan 85
Nightfall. 86

About the Author. 89

He told me that the idea of an animal being "locally extinct" . . . was a difficult concept for him to understand. It's possible, he told me, that the *body* of an animal might not be visible to someone traveling through a certain country, but the animal was still there. In its corporeal form it might be "finished" in a particular place, but it wasn't "gone." . . . If you couldn't see it, I asked, couldn't find its tracks or scat or signs of its feeding, wasn't it "locally extinct"? No, he said. He waved his extended left hand quickly in a sweeping arc. "It's all out there, everywhere."

— Barry Lopez, from *Horizon*

Horses
(Author's Introduction)

Friends of ours who lived along the McKenzie River in southern Oregon hung in their house two Rick Bartow drawings made with charcoal, pastel, and graphite on paper, each with the word "HORSES" scrawled across the bottom; one is titled "Blue Shadow" and the other "Pink Shadow." Both pieces stand 74 x 40 inches and depict a figure with an equine face from which lines drop to suggest a human frame, shoulders, or perhaps a robe. The bodies and ears of each drawing hold much negative space, lightly outlined, although their faces are highly detailed: one has yellow, white, and brown almost cubist patches on its muzzle and forehead as heavier black lines define its eyes, edges, and shape in a more realist manner; blue and charcoal create one-dimensional shading around the head, and two dark handprints sit on each side of its chest. The face of the other follows the same formal pattern but uses several pink pigments and a lighter blue, with less charcoal, to create its lines and shadows.

When we stayed over for a few days each summer, and after talking long into the evening, I often found myself still up, sitting alone, transfixed, trying to figure out how these HORSES worked. Back home from our first visit, I continued to mull over these creatures—at night or when walking my son to school or putting away dishes, they would rise in my mind's eye and we would talk and they would tell me all of what once was: all those species of animal and plant and god and landscape and destruction and climate and kinship and anatomy and question and chaos and era and life and death and myth and metamorphosis and change. In the years that gathered since the onset of these conversations, the McKenzie River Valley burned and our friends moved away and we could no longer travel to their home in the forest. Still the HORSES came to talk, and I steadily transcribed what I learned in a series of notebooks (which I labeled "transmutations") until one morning they said that they too, soon, would go. Afterwards, they said, I should be more able to understand them. When their visits stopped, I began to reread the sketch-data-poems they left and perceived certain facts as to the geological relations of the present to the past inhabitants of their real imagined landscapes. I began to see how the HORSES expressed Darwin's vision as an animistic fact of our everyday environments and bodies. I am publishing a selection of these verses now because they told me to and because I miss them.

of Species

Transmutation 1

Transmutation: Kith and Kin

What did God do while waiting for humans to evolve? Did it walk about, jump over the inland waterways and volcanos, sit under the palms and play hide and seek with the other animals to pass time? Did it check in on all the primates to see how they were coming along? How the mandrills were doing? Did God watch their struggle to speak, take fieldnotes about how their lips moved and tongues twisted? Keep a scrapbook on annual heights and weights? Did it know the precise moment they were to become what they were to become and plan a party for just after? Did it also grieve, then, just a little, when it happened? Or did God wonder what they would be like, wonder what was set in motion? Play out conversations in its mind? Did it think to prepare to teach them how to build a fire and finish a stitch? How did God imagine they would get along? What they would do with all those kids? Did it imagine their bodies colored and shaped? The many ways they could open on purpose or not on purpose, their latches and ways of bending and being put together and taken apart?

Adaptation

       this is the blast, here

Such mutation that matters, all

the whole sum & pith

       all by itself

a spiral, a first somersault

splayed through spine and toes

flung at the coast from the sea

Such petals, what pods & seeds

wheel
       drop what cosmos of

toes and spines and skulls

Craving

Among a push of saplings—
rooted clouds burst

since fusion's first traversing

hushed fire,
gathered, already gathering;

these taut
trunks, clutch of leaves—

The Inheritance of Archaeology

to be of use

to our ancestors

who stepped off from the trees first

picked up a stick,

sticks
        and

started beating everything
                        to death

down and up on what limbs,

eating plums and fleas,

kudus, springbucks,

a clawless otter,

hyenas, a short-necked giraffe, some

brush pigs and pygmy hippos,

similarly different primates

The Rise of Nation States

My neighbor calls it the smell of
freedom

blowtorching my way through weeds
interrupting gravel pathways of

my landscaping

what
also keeps toxins from the watershed.

Spacetime

Not a one, again, to notice

a change in inclination of the Earth's axis
pours into the brine

frazil and shuga cuddle

icebergs trifle & rub
unfamiliar coast

called by no one, the coming of,

called shimmer, called hoist.

A System of Signs, or Its Forebear, Back in the Head of This *Australopithecus*

He looks up from his scratches

sees the Sun

knows it doesn't matter

knows it's removed from a sheath
he hasn't cracked either,

knows it's a sign

for something

he doesn't see
in
a symbolic order,

scratches away.

Coasts

A slope becomes a bluff
A bluff becomes a cave
A cave becomes an arch
An arch becomes a stack
A stack becomes a beach
A beach becomes its surf
Surf becomes salt
Salt becomes sediment
Sediment becomes sleep.

Pearyland

A caribou walks down off Mt. Nordkrone's straight face

follows the meltwater trickling down to the fjord
listens to the poppies turning on their stalks

thinks about the first clothing

its forelegs used for boot uppers and in the palms of mittens
for how they resist abrasion

its calf used for underclothes and boot liners.

Who can know what their dreaming minds want done?
How to get back to this place where you get your body from?

Transmutation 11

Transmutation: Laughter

What did the first laugh sound like? Was it a giggle or a kind of moan? Did it slip out as a surprise? Did the noise spread like a virus? Was it hunted for, after, like a mushroom?

Of Prophets and Prophecies

A boil of clouds breaks
over the mountains like a crocodile

(through bluff and peaks,
the sky that shakes)—

rejoices and does not fear; falls not
as snout and tail, but

sprawls over stacks of feldspar and clay,
the desert pastures,

the fig trees putting on their fruits,
the measured rains in the fall,

the rains that come down
in the spring.

Restored are the years
that the locusts ate,

the cutter-worms, the fire,
the streambeds.

Aubade

For the gleaming a small dark

for the day, plants yielding seeds, and
seed-bearing plants

wild beasts for the grass

for the firmament
a surface for the deep

for the creatures that teem
that move about underneath.

Lucy's Tanka: "I Am Not the Moon"

Not the moon, not
those drops of light

what walks those feet
under dappled night,

what huddles from sight, not
not what rocks

arms crossed
tight,

not yet scattered
meat not meat

meat
not able to make flight.

Interlocutor

What is innocent but the lion's roar?
What is mercy but the eagle that falls on its prey?

Whelp and scatter when calls and trembles
When moths ferry down the rain, down the morning,

All evening, push waves out over the plains,
Flutter before seas among thorns and thirsty—

Sent forth they overwhelm; called back they go dry.
Now it comes now it comes and how stand and

What dismay: the snows heap far above; their
Ways wind, mount, and are lost. There the stones

Make their pacts; the wild ass and ox make league,
Chiefs of the pathless, heirs to the futile moons,

The days that snap off from clouds revolving in
Wonder, the sun that never ceases from rising and

Rest: plunderers of the dust of the fastness, how they
Slaughter—the blossoms made great so just to

Destroy them; the grasses brought forth for to
Grope and stagger. What, then, are strength and

Prudence to a spider? Its cobweb a house only hope
Will dwell in; the trunk it clings to its only prospect,

When fallen, it can decompose; it still sends up
Shoots, though its toes grow old in the ground, it

Leads all to the sound of water. Where come from
Where going, it asks all who tarry.

It answers with shade and striplings.
It spawns hills and heavens alike.

Pantheon

The god of this tree
is the tree
it can touch, its
god the god
of the tree
it touches back.

The *Homo sapiens* Called Isaac

Shifty old eyes

Watch him

withered mumbling man

Watch him

Watch him don't bring a knife.

First Version

In the beginning neither being nor not being was.
No firmament, no air, no on the other side of them
either.

In the beginning there was an egg.
In the beginning the beginning sat for years, sat and sat

and then split asunder, the beginning became—
one half silver, the other gold.

The eggshell that was silver now the ground,
the gold now the sky.

The membrane's top, all wrinkles, now mountains;
the underside now cloud and mist,
the veins marbling out, rivers.

Born from this egg is that yonder star.
Shout and hurrah all creatures all your desires rise up;

shout and hurrah at every rising and return,
sisters, delight, delight him, brothers, delight, delight.

Of Organisms and Not Specimens

The grief of all plants that grip
That reach
      down

Rocks crevice, crack
Till culls & hails

What must bind
What doesn't adore a topple

All that huddles against
Landslides and hurricanes

Slumps, slides,
      falls, flows,
                creeps.

Transmutation 111

Transmutation: Art

What was the first art? Was it an agate found in a wash, carried for its cast and color, useless for murder or cooking? When did hands first seek shapes in wood, see plants as pigments rather than medicine? How did a bone become something to hang from ears? A handle something to hold spirits and geometry? How did they come to crawl on their bellies in the dark to trace their hands on the walls of caverns farther back?

Armaments

Giants who but cannot walk
but by stretching out
but by firing their young out
over the plains in turacos' beaks

covering the wilderness with a
different wilderness, stems and heads
out of sight, to and fro they go,

no cause but for more shadows, no
measure but for how much they swallow.

Homo habilis, in Chorus

Heaps of pygmies & elephant
    scraps
peeled back by bashed out
    skeans—whole
blooms of sweets—when

sisters and brothers
    roar
knee deep in
jackals & hyenas,
    the

clotting dark, scoring
    with obsidian and sticks
the coming bewilderment
    of song.

Of Erosion and Starting Out

A canyon pines for itself

A stream's embrace of what
wants to be there

Banks behind banks below beds cup
beds cup beds as

ash & wild pear grimace

cling to
a north-facing cliff face rushes
at the havoc of jade and

brunswick green—become
a bag for keeping time

a beacon that is that terror at rest
never mistook for anything else.

Like Schools of Fish Wheeling in the Air

250,000 lesser snow geese,

their night voices,

exhausted as if some calamity,

alight for the first or fifth or tenth time

at this intemperate arctic edge where each

took first breath.

What tugs at their minds?

Draws them back to this basin

with hope that the weather will be fair and

their timing good?

The paradox of a breeding colony.

The synchronized confusion of their bodies'

opaque whiteness, the grayer whites

in their translucent wings and

tail feathers—undulating shades that

doubt what the marsh might give

and refuse to tell what happens next.

The *Homo sapiens* Called Ishmael

The dreams of gullies and crevasses
during dry seasons

dregs and dross laud and shout
the arrangements of runoff and rills

the father of rocks borne
from the land of its bearing

rise, lift up, your opened eyes—gather
that drizzle under your skin.

Learning How to See

The cranes
still
in the surf
remind me of nothing

As do the bare silk trees
aloof
thirty steps from the aphotic zone's
foaming fringe.

Mass & Heat

Stories that velocity & color tell
about the precarity of liquids and pieces
suspended in them, syllogisms such that
slacken, permafrost relaxing, warming up,
chunks swimming off, Magellans of
the Moon's Daughter, Bearers of
Landscapes to Landscapes, Bringers-
Forth-of-All-Things who will not
understand an invasive species,
cannot think the forms of
indigenous biomass, the closed
system and its doings, propositions
of the homogenous, a kind of clean.

The *Homo sapiens* Called Rebekah

Tip your lips
your camels' throats a kindness

may we empty and draw
may we trough and run.

Transmutation IV

Transmutation: Bears

When did the bears stop talking? Was it an act of protest or a flash of second sight? Did they run out of words to say or weary of rhetorical gestures? Object to the vagaries of meaning that hung from the tips of their tongues? Or did they decide to refrain from frivolous speech and are still waiting for a subject worthy of their attention? Did they get together and cast votes or did it happen all of a sudden? Are the words just caught in their throats? Do they yet whisper to the briars and marmots when no one else can hear them, converse with the constellations when even the owls are in bed? Was it an embrace of that silence? Do they find the quiet a comfort? Were they only trying to rest the mad rush of their minds, simply turning away from all longings and the incessant churn of such babbles? Do the bears now swim in the ripples of oxygen as it moves across their faces, tickling the hairs inside their ears and noses? Do they sit instead alone under the underbrush, or in a river waiting for salmon, listening to the push back of the boulders? Do they want the companionship of what is wordless? Were they straining to hear the emptiness of thought and keep track of their daydreams, choosing to forget the nuances of bellows and the way the days had turned against them, the sounds of birth and death, arising and falling asleep? Did they see our faults and decide to spare our feelings, waiting for a grace that might yet come in the hush? Do they just prefer looking for berries on the hillsides? Was it then that they began to feel their hearts beat?

A Theory of Tools

      1.

If I crouch like a bird
gradually flap
back, reverse
in my rest that tickling dread.

      2.

Give what a hammerstone gives
of skull, of ligament, of spinal column.

      3.

Underfoot, a dry gully
gathers the crush of summer
broods on the overthrow of the streams below.

Then This *Homo habilis*, the First Rückenfigur

She sits and overlooks &
doesn't think about her death

doesn't think what—

thinks about how sweet

the when

        under tongue & teeth

thinks about the light
not to come

thinks to be still gathered &
to still be squeezed.

Lessons from the Wolverine

They study more than others do, silt and other things
beautiful cobbles—reds, grays, greens, browns.

The strange way they have when they hurry along
that's how you know them when they walk like that.

The way you know fish are in a river
they carry their culture in their heads.

They know where to find a story's boundary
they know not to look for the whole of it.

Where they have made marks on the ground from dancing
or a little house.

Up there they said it's not a good place for us
we don't go there now, we don't go up there too much.

One of Some *Homo habilis*

A locust of flamingoes, and
the shallows of the beanstalk lake,

four in the foreground step back
for each step he takes;

he knows how little distance he needs,
how much they require to take flight,

of
the molt of patience somewhat less,

measured in the scant between
skulk and dash, and

the whole mob's shuddering,
spasms of jubilation

their wild amble to stain the sun, the
shoals

all lifted and gone—he
left under on the mudflats, back

to searching for eggs, dreaming of
the feel of feathers between his hands.

Climate-lapse

the sky thins

Continents calve
                like glaciers

Swamps sink in savannah

The Origin of Biography (*Homo georgicus*)

As a girl she scarred her face
climbing a fruit tree, then

there were few in the lowlands,
nevertheless, sons and daughters, their

daughters and sons, mostly
outlived but spreading,

because she knew when to move,
which trails to follow

because
she knew where to find good water,

the mate who went hunting and
didn't come home,

all the tender ones, kept
together

as the stratosphere ties
its eyes to its waist,

because she knew how tendrils
could be cords for packing.

Not Quite Metamorphosis

then pause, then flit, then

away,

away,

away

Second Version

In the beginning there was water.
Water is what was everywhere.
That is how it was—just a sea,
wide and stretched in all directions
over everything.

In this watery world lived the otter,
hither and thither with its thick tail
and webbed feet; its cousin too, the
beaver, thick furred, builder of lodges
in which to live and cover its young.

Past chewed logs slid the muskrat, also—
sculling like a snake; under and over
went the bull trout and other fish and
plovers that love the waves and ripples,
strutting ducks and chorales of geese.

But there were no people.

Homo georgicus Continued—
Her at a Vanishing Point

A tempest in her brain
A glimpse walking forward

like a boy, at first, when
seen at the size of the sun

then scarred and wind slapped
the old woman,

fixed like that,
like she wore two skins, the first

up in ripples under the outer
pushing down on

her nape and ribs, as
closer, almost foreign,

she steps
to press that part of the plant that

could be swallowed
through her palm,

(all the torrent of her fingers), set
into that tumult and wonder

stretching out the one head
inside the other.

Transmutation V

Transmutation: Rites

What was the first funeral like? Did they find a natural fissure to close with sediment or did they dig, and were the tools taboo for some? Did they curl the body in on itself when they placed it in the pit? Did they wrap it in a cloth or cover it with vegetation? Were they worried about scavengers? Did they fear she needed more food or amulets or pelts? Who painted the body with red ocher? How long before they begin to include jewelry, feathers, or colored shells? When did they start to mark the graves with shale slabs or intricately carved poles and how did these signs change the landscape, its meaning and where they could walk without a skip? When did they begin to stand quiet and when did they start to sing? To whom did it matter and for what length of days or generations?

A Dream of Empire

What is the ambition of grasses?
What dreams as they throng
with the winter in abeyance?

The *Homo sapiens* Called Jacob

And, look

come upon, and look,

for the night
a stone of the place and put, lay down

And, look

a ramp set against the marl
with its top reach

going up and coming down, and look,

the land and its dust
dwells
in the land of its father's sojournings

And, look
And look

where you gone, brought back
where you haven

where quail and dredge,
withdraw and insist,

glance and peck.

Sister of Needles

Willows know what they are,
ravens are very similar, but
are never frightened
by the weight of flight.

Psalms

The earth belongs to fire, the earth and everything in it,

A likeness of air, matter, and sun,
it ambles and runs, hails the luxuriant land, vows

Increase and spread, flames that walk blameless and
do not slander with tongues on bark and prairie, lick

Briar and tangle, trace up the rungs, vault to pinnacle
limbs, caper from crown to crown, smolder below the
surface of dry wetlands,

See now the embers float and sally forth—spot and
settle far ahead—oh the fire takes its weather with it,

Plumes of heat and turbulence shudder grays, tower
in anvil shape, shed lightening without rain,

Whirlwinds of rainbow shreds hurl themselves
against the foothills' inky mantle and valleys baying,

Hear the peaks scurry, lie down in their sleep, their
cataracts heave, their courses roil and roar with

Debris, their high meadows catacombs without
lids, such pyres they need not brides, like lions that

Long for prey, ravenous counters of bones casting
their eyes over the open plains, their vows these fires

Do not revoke, they do not stumble or take bribes, as
spinney unto spinney calls out, as the wild ox

Dances and totters to voices of boiling cedars whose
knowledge of fire does not abate, hear

The wisdom of fire: what will not see the bog's
footings? All wear their way to the mire's foundation
to make it their dwelling place,

When sap turns to amber, when the weald beholds
the wakes of desolation, no tears tumble forth, all

Alike perish and abandon their portions to what
follows, the flowers' splendor is for them alone, at

Cockcrow they flourish and by roost they shrivel under
smoke, in a breath, merest breath and are gone—the
muck is their home forever;

But hold, be still, do not gargle lamentations, come
whelps and saplings, listen—the
wilderness's grasp of fire you will harken:

To the beasts of the forest the beasts belong, herds
on the thousand crags know their numbers, every bird

On the wing knows its kin, for the loam is the loam's
and its fullness, when streams run dry thunder answers

From its hiding place, when the moon wanes it's a
festival for the faint, the swallow builds an alter for its

Fledglings and their throats lift vows and blessings,
when the land burns it offers itself back to its soil, the

Canopy opens for glimmers tumble down and
lupines flourish and caterpillars weave their

Cocoons, a stand thinned of thirsty shrubs gives more
cheer & spread, trees bear fruit as their profession, their

Leaves do not wither, only watch the murmur of
flames leap from rampart to rampart

Reach the buzzards dangling from the heavens,

Sweep out to dolphin pods, those riders of waves,
their spouts a drizzle dappling the swells,

Now the fire kisses the dead foliage along the ground
and the acres nuzzle sprouts and shoots, pinecones

Turn out seeds for sowing, bees clothe the boulders
and brambles until they are sated with honey,

Pitch cankers and bark beetles, the great
despoilers, parish in the flames, always the rivers

Clap gladly before their tributaries, they guide
themselves through valleys flush with shadows and

Do not wander, they get themselves to the sea,
get and give their bodies to its saturation, fall

Together with glee, the crags in their
rapids and breakers are their bastions, their choir

Lifting up songs of thanksgiving: sing gladly, all
spates and pastures, sing gladly

Righteous lilies and scrub oak who love the fire and
flames, for what flourishes, praise is befitting, glory,

Glory, their eyes have seen it, glory, glory may
fire's peace rage until the globe liquefies inside its star.

The Love of Deserts

artifacts of light

grains dune

billows in billions
each itself rubs, each itself sweeps

Some *Homo georgicus* Going Here and There

When the weather turns colder,
follow the animals

stay in the lowlands until the sycamores bend sweet and
bats swarm—swing monsoons from their tails—then

disperse into the highlands, leave
the closer bright behind;

go back after the mornings grow brittle,
fit each step to the wales of hooves and sharper feet.

Boxing the Compass

The horizon sits on the horizon itself

The horizon sits itself on the horizon

Itself the horizon sits itself on the horizon itself

The horizon sits on itself

The horizon itself sits on the horizon itself

Itself the horizon sits on the horizon

Sit horizon on the horizon itself

The horizon itself sits on itself

Itself the horizon sits on the horizon itself

The horizon sits on itself the horizon

The horizon sits itself on the horizon itself

The Discovery of Grief (*Homo georgicus*)

The old woman rocks
her back and forth, hums

puts
some cherries in her mouth

there humming all
among all the little ones

answering
may we all be comforted.

Transmutation VI

Transmutation: Music

Was the first music a mistake, the accident of hitting stick against stick, or hand against hand or hide or rock or reed? How long before a meal became a drum? How long before a voice became a pitch or a whistle that startled and tried to join the crows?

Tectonic Shifts

Plates afloat and piles of dust and moisture
        compounded

Leap, speckled pebble lift, rise higher,
        smash and shake

Awake, awake: look awry, look new.

A Family Tree (*Homo pekinensis*)

At their backs partially butchered

old man
stop the wind

anchor other skins

stiffen & cup
embers and limbs

against a winter
more wanton

than a cave
thinned of fingers

&
little
legs

nibble

while nothing pours in.

In Place of an Altar

Long married the trees, the parrots, and the bruising hour
Always asunder those three and those peculiar, curious feet.

Thresholds

Bury the bones of bears
place their skulls in trees

Throw back the bones of fish
turn your eyes, do not see them reach,
pull back on their skins

Drill the teeth of seals
suffer the ocean
to wear your collar on a string.

Third Version

At first only darkness unseen in the dark.
Alone it was alive.

Then it came to pass a terrible stomach pain,
pains that grew and grew

until finally up vomited the Sun.

Now the world was brightened each day;

the heat caused much dew to float—
the breeze to become some thunderheads

the reefs and sandbanks to ring joy, to raise thanks.

*

Then it came to pass once again a
terrible stomach pain,

pains that grew and grew until finally up
vomited the Moon and the stars.

Now the world was brightened each night.
Moon's rays and stars' lights.

*

Then it came to pass again terrible
stomach pains, pains that grew and grew

until finally up vomited the first
living creatures: up came the leopard; up

came the crested eagle; up the minnow fish,
the crocodile, who created the iguana who

created all in the forests and in the fields.
Up vomited the tortoise,

the white heron, as beautiful as
the leopard was deadly and quick, and

who created all the flocks that fly. Up
came the beetles and goats who created

the insects and horned animals each.

*

Then once again it came to pass again such
terrible stomach pains,

a pain that grew and grew until finally up
vomited the first human beings

who began to wiggle and run about, who first
split open the fire that lives in every stock

and carried it home, first looked for wonder in
the sky and in the fruits, nuts, and grains,

in the humors in their hearts that were their own,
in their eyes and ears, nose and tongue.

The *Homo sapiens* Called Rachel

Be not incensed, she says,
she says for what is upon me, as it does,

Rummaged, her rummaged and
rummaged about,

Not found, found not out, felling
as she fled.

Why Do Islands Swim?

A tooth in a hill is a plow

A fern in a cliff a hoe

A mountain on a plateau such a raft

Canoes to cut, to pitch and yaw

across the sea

Their beaches heave away, heave up

away up on their eventual beach.

Understory

Green all morning
with hope they'll be green tomorrow
the limb sits among other limbs.

Transmutation VII

Transmutation: History

What was the first history? Who recalled it and for what reason? Did it recount a long walk into the interior? Was it a winter when all the newborns perished or a springtime when a two-headed kite nested nearby? What did they agree counted as a record? Were they hoping to explain a string of springs at the bottom of foothills and windbreaks across the plateau? Was it an ache to understand their grandmothers, what made them hate and what made them abandon and light out from far away? Did they argue about why it mattered? With what materials did they share their ideas and interpretations? Where did they decide to store these reeds or rocks or recitals? Was it a place or was it all in their heads?

Animals That Did Not Make It into the Ark

The end of all flesh is come,
for the earth fills with the outrage of the earth

and those what could not count
not among them who float

on the wellsprings and the casements
confounded as what they gobble:

Long-beaked Echidnas,
Smilodons and the Skinny Shrew,

a tiny snail called a Kimberella,
Terror Birds that crushed skulls like melons,

all Bambiraptors and Dragons,
the simple Tyrannosaurus rex;

also the Ground Sloth, also
the Walking Worm,

a Parasaurolophus who sung to the waves,
Griffins, Glyptodons, and every shrub;

include the Bear-dog, Bigfoots,
miniature crocodiles and zombie ants,

Velociraptors carving rain,
a rat the size of a bull, Wonderchickens,

how they surge
waterlogged, how they speculate.

Crow's Side of the Tale, pastel, graphite on paper by Rick Bartow, 1991

Alight in this gully

I watch
the moon watch right back;

it too must wonder
the number of eyes that will

rise and crumble before
it falls

faint
to fill

the cleft from where it once
jumped,

where I now sit.

The *Homo sapiens* Called Leah

Who more despised by such wanters of sons?
Who with a womb more opened?

Nocturne

Cuckoo leave my ears alone;
cease your soothsaying—I

already feel the disinvitation of
sod and scrub. I

will fill your beak
with caterpillars and katydids &

turn my feet from your groves
in the morning

if I can ever get my head
to bed

again.

Virgil's 81st Grandson Sits in the Tundra

The silent arrival of caribou in an otherwise empty landscape

The long crouch at a seal hole until prey surfaces

When a lead finally closes

When a huge piece of sheet ice surges hundreds of feet inland

While water bears migrate over the canyons of jade-green vegetation

While a film of moisture coats a bit of moss on a stone nestled in other mosses

Additional Mammals

Before hedgerows or shelterbelts

the waste that creates fertile land,
the accumulation of abraded earth,

not the yearning for cut and plow,
But not not the desire for them either,

just indifference & oblivion
as the breeze buries all alike.

Minyan

A precipice of compressed skeletons of
marine microorganisms and coral

dreams of becoming gypsum,
dissolving in rainwater, escaping

as an incombustible gas; wear away,
it sings, avoid the curse of marble,

in time, all who live
shiver, will be sheltered, with all creatures
      we daven.

Nightfall

Water beneath and water atop

currents swarm with the swarm of

who wash, who drift
                      —another day.

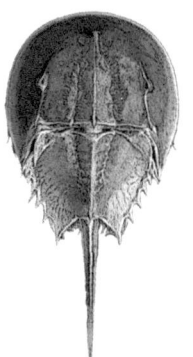

ABOUT THE AUTHOR

JOEL BETTRIDGE is the author of four other books of poetry, *Ligatures* (Dos Madres 2019), *The Public Life of Chemistry* (The Cultural Society 2018), *Presocratic Blues* (Chax 2009), and *That Abrupt Here* (The Cultural Society 2007), as well as two critical studies, *Avant-Garde Pieties: Aesthetics, Race, and the Renewal of Innovative Poetics* (Routledge 2018) and *Reading as Belief: Language Writing, Poetics, Faith* (Palgrave 2009). He co-edited *Ronald Johnson: Life and Works* (The National Poetry Foundation 2008). He is Professor of English at Portland State University.

OTHER BOOKS BY JOEL BETTRIDGE
PUBLISHED BY DOS MADRES PRESS

LIGATURES (2019)

FOR THE FULL DOS MADRES PRESS CATALOG:
www.dosmadres.com

Printed by Libri Plureos GmbH in Hamburg, Germany